C000273152

EASTBOURNE

THROUGH TIME

Kevin Gordon

AMBERLEY PUBLISHING

*I would like to dedicate this book to my family past and present,
particularly my long suffering wife, Mandy.*

*I would also like to thank Lawrence and Pat Stevens for permission to use
the pictures on pages 10 and 12 and for sparking my interest in history
many years ago.*

First published 2010

Amberley Publishing Plc
Cirencester Road, Chalford,
Stroud, Gloucestershire, GL6 8PE

www.amberley-books.com

Copyright © Kevin Gordon, 2010

The right of Kevin Gordon to be identified as the
Author of this work has been asserted in accordance
with the Copyrights, Designs and Patents Act 1988.

ISBN 978 1 84868 133 0

All rights reserved. No part of this book may be
reprinted or reproduced or utilised in any form
or by any electronic, mechanical or other means,
now known or hereafter invented, including
photocopying and recording, or in any information
storage or retrieval system, without the permission
in writing from the Publishers.

British Library Cataloguing in Publication Data.
A catalogue record for this book is available from
the British Library.

Typeset in 9.5pt on 12pt Celeste.
Typesetting by Amberley Publishing.
Printed in the UK.

Introduction

Elegant spot of the sunny South
A mansion enclosed with hills round about
Surrounded by beauty and foliage green
To equal its splendour can never be seen
Behold where you may it is pleasant and bright
Of things that recruit both the health and the sight
Undone from the city you can here find rest
Refreshed by the breezes that blow from the west
New vigour obtained by a stroll near the sea
Empress of the South let its name ever be!

This was an acrostic poem written in 1933 Ebenezer Roberts to mark the jubilee of Eastbourne becoming a borough in 1883. Ebenezer was my great grandfather (see page 54) who also has a long lasting love of this evergreen town on the south coast. By all accounts he was a strict and deeply religious man who regularly preached at local churches, was a senior Oddfellow, wrote poetry and was the Captain of the Bonfire Society at St Mary's, Old Town.

Generations of my family were born, lived and worked in Eastbourne which has many happy memories for me, one of my earliest being the excitement of watching the Eastbourne lifeboat being pushed into the sea during stormy weather from the lifeboat station. I recall the fun of bumping along to the Crumbles on the tiny Eastbourne trams (page 21) and winkling and rockpooling at Holywell. I clearly remember the swarms of mods and rockers motorcycling through the town in the sixties and also the terrible fire in 1970 which nearly destroyed the pier. At Christmas the family would stroll along the prom to walk off the Christmas pud and listen to the band. This photograph shows me in 1966 in one such yuletide walk.

Eastbourne is a genteel resort with none of the glitz, glamour and 'kiss-me-quickness' of other seaside towns; even today there are no shops or amusement arcades along the seafront. Attracted by the warm weather (it is regularly the sunniest place on mainland Britain), its large retired

community has led some people to call Eastbourne 'Zimmerland' but if you stroll along the long parades you will find that it is also a family resort with much to offer for younger people including plenty of clubs and bars for younger adults. The town has hotels to suit all pockets, can boast of an important new art gallery, theatres, a top sporting venue and is still surrounded by beautiful downland and coastal scenery. What better place to live or spend a holiday?

What would Ebenezer think of the Eastbourne of the twentieth century? Much of the town has changed beyond recognition and unfortunately he died during the Second World War having witnessed the destruction of many beautiful buildings caused by the many air raids.

However, I like to think that Ebenezer would be comforted to see that much of old Eastbourne, although modernised, still remains recognisable today, particularly along the seafront and in at Meads.

I hope that the following pages show that my Great grandfather Ebenezer was right – Eastbourne is still the Empress of the South!

Kevin Gordon
July 2010

CHAPTER 1

Old Town

The Origins of Eastbourne

This pond in Motcombe Gardens is the source of the Bourne Stream which gives Eastbourne its name. The springs here were known in Saxon times and were not only a source of water for Motcombe Farm, the building shown here, but also growing reeds to make baskets. The building on the left with the tall chimney is Motcombe Swimming Baths. The pond was lined and enclosed in 1857 and the stream that leaves the pond flows behind houses in the Goffs and once flowed into a Mill Pond near the junction of Southdown Road. The lead figure of Neptune was moved to this location from the Mill Pond.

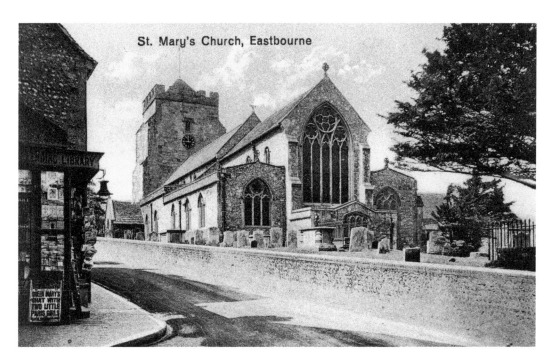

St. Mary's Church, Eastbourne

St Mary's Church

The solid twelfth century church is full of interest and well worth a visit. It was originally dedicated to St Michael and has many Norman features including the chancel arch which has dogtooth carving. The south wall has a memorial to Henry Lushington whose 'singular merits and singular sufferings cannot fail to endear him to posterity'. He joined the East India Company aged 16 and the memorial lists his adventures when he was thrown into the Black Hole of Calcutta. 146 were imprisoned but only Henry and 22 other survived.

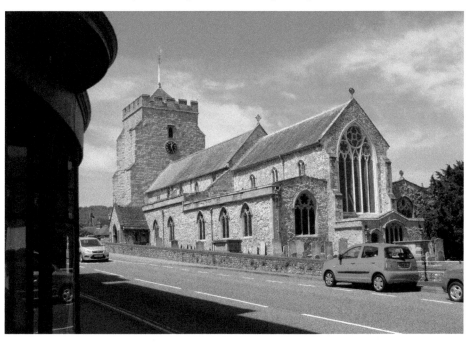

The Church Tower

The impressive church tower dates from the fourteenth century and is of Eastbourne greensand which would have been quarried from a site near to the pier. It contains six bells cast in 1651 and two dated 1818. The passageway connecting the church and the Old Parsonage was built as a memorial to the dead of the First World War. It is interesting to see that in the past 100 years the graveyard has been levelled and many old tombs cleared.

The Old Parsonage

Almost abutting the north side of St Mary's Church, the Old Parsonage was probably erected for Hugh Rolfe in the first half of the sixteenth century and remains a good example of Tudor architecture. It was originally the Rectory Manor House and was also called the 'Nether Inn' and consisted of a large hall with a buttery and pantry at the north end and a solar (living room) at the south end. The building was later converted into three cottages but was presented to the parish by the Duke of Devonshire. The Old Parsonage was restored after the First War War and became a listed building in May 1949.

The Jesus House

A collection of medieval buildings once stood in the area to the north of St Mary's Church. One was the 'Jesus House', which was probably run by a religious brotherhood. The 1878 directory shows that there as also a toy repository here and Kolassy House. (Probably named after Mount Kailassy said to be the home of the Hindu gods and used for house names in India). In the late seventies I was one of a group of enthusiastic local people who helped to excavate the area under local archaeologists Lawrence and Pat Stevens. I recall the fear and excitement in being lowered down ancient wells to retrieve items which had not seen light of day for hundreds of years. Amongst the items found on the site were thirteenth century pottery and a rare Spanish drug jar dating from the fifteenth century. The area is now occupied by St Mary's Court retirement home.

The High Street

Although the road here has been widened, the scene has not changed. The shop on the right later became the Regents Cinema. The red and white brick building on the left is now a pizza takeaway but started life as a brewery and for many years was a wine merchant's. On the side of the building is one of the last remaining Victorian wall-mounted post-boxes.

The Star

In the early 1800s this site was occupied by Mr Mandy's slaughterhouse. The two cottages, 22 and 20, High Street were probably built at the same time. Number 22 is a tile hung brick built house but 20 is faced with boulders (the local name for stones taken from the beach). The Star Brewery was established here in 1777 and soon dominated the site. The last pint of Star Ale was brewed here in September 1967 and shortly afterwards the brewery and these cottages were demolished. Then the site was purchased by Tesco and in May 1980 they gave permission for local archaeologists Lawrence and Pat Stevens to excavate the area. A Waitrose supermarket now occupies the site.

The Manor House

The Manor House was built for the Revd Henry Lushington who, from 1734 to 1779, was vicar of Eastbourne. In 1819 it was described as being a 'superior brick mansion having good gardens and commanding extensive sea views'. In 1922 the house and grounds were purchased by the Corporation and the following year the Manor House was used to display a collection of art left by Alderman John Towner, becoming the Towner Art Gallery. In 2009 the Towner Gallery moved to a smart new building alongside the Congress Theatre (see page 79). The installation that now sits in front of the building is called '4,000 Tides' by David Nash and is constructed from recycled oak groynes from the seafront.

The Lamb Hotel, Eastbourne

The Lamb Inn

Although dating from the sixteenth century, there has probably been an inn here for much longer. It was a coaching inn and until 1875 the only licensed place of entertainment in the town with theatrical productions in the Assembly Room at the back of the building. The plaster on the front of the building was removed in 1912. This was a regular haunt for me when I lived nearby and it still serves a good pint of Harvey's and a filling meal. If you are lucky the landlord may even take you downstairs to see the beautiful vaulted medieval cellars.

Summerdown Camp

In 1914, 50 acres of land was set aside to the west of the East Dean Road to build a hutted military camp. In April 1915 the first convalescents arrived. Because of their uniform, these men were known locally as 'Blue Boys'. My great-great uncle, Bertie Bennett was a local printer and published the camp magazine for several years. Concerts and outings (see page 96) were arranged for these men to try to get them over the horrors of the trenches. Today Summerdown Road and Old Camp Lane are sited on the old camp.

Old Town Post Office
Until 1880 the post office was in a small cottage in Ocklynge Road to the rear of the Lamb Inn. The postmaster at this time was John Payne and after his death his wife Hannah became the official postmistress. She remained when the office moved to Star Lane, shown above. The large tower in the background belonged to the Star Brewery. Today the post office has returned to Ocklynge Road but is now on the corner of Crown Street.

CHAPTER 2

Eastern Parades

Previous page: Royal Parade looking east towards the Redoubt Fortress.

The Stade

The area between the Redoubt and the pier has always been used for Eastbourne's beach-hauled fishing fleet. Known as 'The Stade' and later 'Sea-Houses' it was the working base of a hardy group of fishermen. My friend and former police colleague Ted Hide has written comprehensive books about the seafaring men of the town. The picture below shows fishing boats registered at Rye (RX) and Newhaven (NN).

The Redoubt

Built to home over 200 soldiers to counter the Napoleonic threat, the Redoubt has since housed a model village, an aquarium and more recently a military museum. In 1996 Southern Water built a Waste Water Works further along the coast, basing the design on the old Redoubt defences. The works treat 74 million litres of water a day. In recent years there have been reports of hauntings – strangely not at the old fortress – but at the new water works!

Parade Bowling Club

There are several active bowling clubs in Eastbourne. The Parade Club started in the 1920s near the Redoubt Fortress and one its first presidents was Mr R. C. Best. This postcard is dated 1928 but I am not sure who the club are playing against. The dress code was not as strict as today although headwear seems compulsory. When the new picture was taken their opponents were from Herstmonceux Bowling Club.

Joy Rides

From 1953 to 1969 a miniature tramway ran on a 2 foot gauge track between Princess Park and the Crumbles (the terminus was where the Sovereign Swimming Centre is now located). Tram number 6, shown here in 1960, was built in 1954 in Barnet, North London by the Lancaster Electrical Company which specialised in making milk floats. My mum and I are in the foreground. Not far away a new form of transport has appeared – a small fleet of Quadricycles, the first at an English seaside resort, first took to the roads in 2009. Ride'n'Joy is run by Pauline Allen from her base near the Redoubt Fortress.

Gilbert Lake, Princess Park, Eastbourne

Gilbert Lake, Princes Park

In 1906 Mr Carew Gilbert-Davis gave 28 acres of the Crumbles to the people of Eastbourne. Unemployed men from the town were used to top the shingle with ballast and soil and create a lake. Originally the area was known as the 'Gilbert Recreation Ground' but when the Duke of Windsor planted a tree here in June 1931 the name was changed to Princes Park. As a boy I recall visiting Gilbert Lake to see the model yachts and power boats which are still regularly raced over the lake by a local club. I also enjoyed playing on the pedalos, pedalling furiously across the water between fleeing swans. Today the lake is called Crumbles Lake and the park is the home to Eastbourne United Football Club as well as a Bowls Club, athletics and cycle track.

Royal Parade

The road stretches from this point to the Crumbles and was built following the passing of the Eastbourne Improvement Act of 1879 which allowed the council to purchase the land and build a sea wall, promenade and road. The project cost £48,000 and the road was eventually opened by the Prince of Wales (later Edward VII) in 1884. The Royal Marine Hotel has been replaced with Metropole Court but the other hotels have remained.

Sea Houses Square

Marine Road runs towards Christ Church which can just be seen in both views. The water fountain which can be seen on the left was installed here ten years ago having previously been located near to the Leaf Hall. It was donated to the town in 1865 by a Mrs Curling and soon became a sort of 'speakers' corner. Fusciardi's Ice Cream Parlour has been providing delicious ices (try their honeycomb flavour!) since I was a lad.

Marine Gardens

Little has changed since this view was taken in the 1930s when Fusciardi's was the Pololi Café. The railings around the gardens would have been removed during the Second World War to help the war effort. Although some railings were used to re-enforce concrete for pill boxes, much of it was unusable and dumped in the North Sea.

The Albion and Albemarle

Now a Travelodge, the Albion was built in 1821 as a home for the Earl of Ashburnham. It was the first house in Eastbourne to use electricity and the first to have a telephone installed (Telephone: Eastbourne 1). The well-proportioned Albermarle Hotel was previously the Anchor Hotel. Regency House, with the blue verandas, was built in 1840 and has Doric columns supporting the balconies and bay windows.

Queens Gardens

2,000 years ago this was the site of a Roman Villa with a pavement bath. It was discovered in 1712. The Queens Hotel was built in 1880 by Henry Currey (1820-1900) possibly to create a visual barrier between the posh hotels of Grand Parade and the cheaper establishments to the east. Indeed until 1898 there was no continuous road here, just steps that led down to Marine Parade. The Belle Vue Hotel to the left of the Queens was built in the mid nineteenth century and is now a listed building.

Pier Entrance, Eastbourne.

Eastbourne Pier

Designed by the marine architect Eugenius Birch (1818-1884) and opened in 1870, Eastbourne pier is 1,000 feet long. The entrance to the pier originally had two round kiosks but these were replaced in 1912 by the ones shown here. The left hand kiosk was a Maynard's shop and the one to the right a booking point for Chapman's Charabanc tours. The central building was a pay-kiosk (2d) but today the pier is free and is still a popular attraction.

Band Stand & Pavilion Pier Eastbourne.

E 114

Pier Theatre and Bandstand

The first theatre was built for £250 in 1888 and could accommodate 400 people. It was replaced in 1899 by a building which also provided café's, bars and the pier offices but this was burnt down in 1970 by a disgruntled employee. For over 100 years there has been a camera obscura on the top of the building which was once the largest in the country. The delicate pier bandstand was moved here from the shoreward end in the 1870s.

2ⁿᵈ Royal Sussex Regt Memorial
Eastbourne

Royal Sussex Regiment Memorial

The statue of a young soldier is the memorial
the those of the Royal Sussex regiment who
were killed in Malta, Egypt and India between
1882 and 1902. It was unveiled in the presence
of a huge crowd on 7 February 1907. In
2007 another member of the regiment was
honoured when a blue plaque was raised to
his memory in Greys Road. Company Sergeant
Major Nelson Victor Carter was posthumously
awarded the Victoria Cross for his bravery in
France in 1916.

CHAPTER 3

West of the Pier

THE PIER AND FRONT. EASTBOURNE

The Burlington and the Claremont Hotels
These hotels to the left of the picture form part of the best building range in Eastbourne. They were built between 1851 and 1855 and were listed in 1949. The early view dates from about 1901 when the only attraction on the pier appears to be the cigarette machine in the foreground.

Eastbourne.

Lower Parade and Yacht.

Towards the Wish Tower

The yacht in the foreground is the *Britannia*, owned by Ben Bates, which provided pleasure trips off Eastbourne between 1890 and 1906 when it was replaced by the *Skylark*. Apart from the bandstand (and fewer holidaymakers) the scene has hardly changed in over a hundred years.

The Bathing Machine

This curious movable beach hut was probably invented in Scarborough in the 1750s and in 1771 the Scottish novelist Tobias Smollett (1721-1771) described how to use them – "The bather ascends into the wooden compartment by wooden steps, shuts himself in and begins to undress while the attendant yolkes a horse to the end next the sea and draws the carriage forwards till the surface of the water is on a level with the floor. The horse is then fixed to the other end and the person, being stripped, opens the door and plunges headlong into the water." During the summer months an old bathing machine is displayed outside the Langham Hotel.

The Bandstand

Built to replace an earlier structure called the Birdcage, the bandstand could seat 3,000 people. It was opened by the Lord Lieutenant of Sussex, Charles Wyndham, Lord Leconfield (1872-1952) on 5 August 1935. Today the bandstand continues to provide concerts to entertain residents and visitors throughout the year.

THE WISH TOWER, EASTBOURNE. 1007.

The Wish Tower

Martello Tower 73 is the last but one in a series of Napoleonic Forts built along the south coast during the French invasion threat of the early nineteenth century. The tower is named after the "wish" or "wash", a marshy area of land that once surrounded it. Apart from the style of cars, the coastline, buildings and even the flowerbeds remain unchanged.

The Lifeboat House

In 1897 William Terriss, a popular actor, was murdered at the stage door of the Adelphi Theatre in London. The *Daily Telegraph* organised a memorial fund for him which in 1899 was used to build a boathouse for the Eastbourne Lifeboat. In 1902 a new lifeboat house was built near the Redoubt Fortress and in 1937 Ellaline Terriss, the actor's daughter, reopened the Terriss memorial as the country's first lifeboat museum.

The Duke of Devonshire

The statue of the 8th Duke of Devonshire still looks out over the Western Lawns and the Landsdown Hotel. Spencer Cavendish (1833-1908) was the leader of the Liberal Party from 1875 to 1880 and turned down the job of Prime Minister on no less than three occasions. He was Mayor of Eastbourne from 1897-1898 and given the freedom of the town in 1903, and his statue by Alfred Drury was unveiled in 1910.

CHAPTER 4

Meads

Holywell Village

Pronounced 'Hollywell' this hamlet was home to fishermen and men who worked in the lime kilns nearby. The building in the foreground is the pumping station for the Eastbourne Waterworks Company. Today the village has gone but the beach is still popular with visitors. The colourful flower display was designed by children from the nearby St John's Primary School in Meads.

Holywell Retreat

Unemployed men were used to convert the Gore Chalk Pit into a formal gardens in 1904. The scheme cost just £400. In 1922 the old pit was renamed the Italian Gardens and a raised walkway was built. This still takes visitors around the back of the gardens which provide a secluded spot for holidaymakers to relax.

EASTBOURNE FROM FOOT OF BEACHY HEAD SHOWING HELEN GARDEN. 1720.

Helen Gardens

In 1930, Mrs Helen Hornby-Lewis left £10,000 to the council to create a garden and putting green. This can be seen behind the buildings of St Bede's School in the foreground. Dolphin Court to the left and the ugly 62m tall South Cliff Tower are the main differences in the view.

Holywell Beach

On a gloomy day in March 1935 King George V and Queen Mary visited Eastbourne and rested in beach chalet number 2 which can be seen in the centre of this view. Today a plaque commemorates the event. The South Cliff Tower built in 1966 peeks above the tree line.

The Tea Chalet, Holywell, Eastbourne.

Holywell Café

In 1921 Eastbourne Borough Council erected a tea chalet at Holywell. This is still a popular place to eat and is also the terminus for the trackless Dotto Train. A building nearby was once housed the English end of the cross-channel telephone cable.

Meads

The bicycle on the left is outside O'Hara's butcher's. The building in the centre of the view, just beyond the turning for Derwent Road was built on the site of the original Ship Inn in 1600 but later resited (see page 49). Matlock Road on the right leads to Meads Village.

Meads Street

This shows Meads Street at the junction of Dalton Road. In the old picture Hammick's bakery occupies the shop on the corner which is now a curio shop called Emma Chisset – not the name of the owner but a play on the words "How much is it?" The next premises is an ironmongery then run by Harold Parker and then Potter's fishmonger's. The last shop is Meads Library which published this view dating from 1919. Today these premises are occupied by an art framer's, dentist and hair and beauty salons.

EASTBOURNE MEAD'S VILLAGE.

52923

Meads Village
This delightful square of Victorian houses with garden plots in the centre, was built in 1894 by George Ambrose Wallis (1840-1895). He was the local agent for the Duke of Devonshire and became Eastbourne's first mayor in November 1883.

All Saurts Convalescent Home. Eastbourne.

All Saints

All Saints Convalescent Hospital took two years to construct and was formally opened on 19 July 1869 by the Bishop of Winchester. The Bishop of Chichester had been invited to conduct the ceremony but declined as he was concerned that the new establishment was 'too Catholic'. The large chapel to the right was completed in 1874. Both buildings were designed by Henry Woodyer (1816-1896) in the gothic revival style. The hospital has now been converted into stylish apartments.

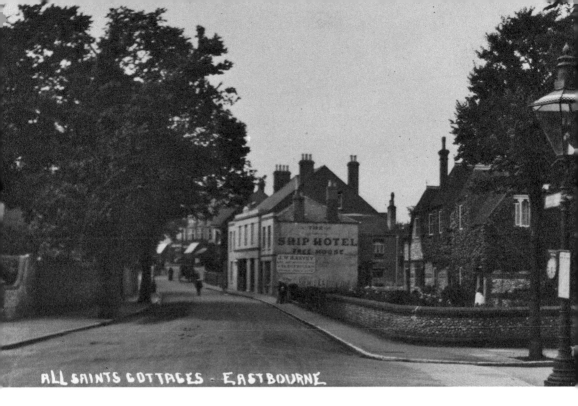

ALL SAINTS COTTAGES - EASTBOURNE

The Ship Inn

In the 1970s, I kept a list of all the Eastbourne pubs I visited. The entry for the Ship reads *"great pub despite outside toilets – lots of cats, dogs and female students"*. St Mary's Cottages on the right have now been replaced by Meads Court. It was between here and the railway station that the worlds first municipal bus service first ran on 12 April 1903.

Western-Parade & Beachy Head, Eastbourne

The Western Parades

William Cavendish, the 7th Duke of Devonshire (1808-1891) funded the creation of the Western Parades, a section of which is named Duke's Drive in his honour. In the 1880s, 400,000 cubic yards of chalk and stone were removed to form the terracing shown here.

CHAPTER 5

Streets

Victoria Drive

This road was named after Queen Victoria shortly after her death in 1901. It was the site chosen by Eastbourne Corporation to build the first council houses in the town. In 1925 some of these houses were used as police houses.

Princess Alice Memorial Hospital, Eastbourne. 444.

Upper Avenue

The Princess Alice Hospital was the general hospital for Eastbourne and was opened in June 1883 by the Prince and Princess of Wales. So many people turned up for this event that a detachment of Dragoon Guards were deployed for crowd control duties. The hospital has now been demolished to make way for The Hawthorns retirement home.

Taddington Road

Taddington is a village in Derbyshire, part of the estate of the Duke of Devonshire. It was at number 15 (a house called Beulah) that my great grandparents, Ebenezer and Bessie Roberts lived. They are seen here in the parlour of the house in 1930.

Victoria Place

This is the seaward end of Terminus Road. This was once the location of the Royal Victoria Baths which boasted hot sea water baths for 1/6d. The building on the right is the Burlington Hotel built in 1851. Inside, Bertie's Bar was a popular venue in the 1970s.

Trinity Trees

This road was previously called Shady Lane and then Seaside Road. When Trinity Church was built here in 1838 the name changed again. The building on the left was Togni and Ferrari's Café but later became Beale's department store and finally the Co-op. A coach and four is passing John Nix jewellers at 6, Terminus Road.

South Street

The steeple of St Saviour's was completed in 1872, five years after the church was consecrated. At the corner of South Street and Cornfield Road is H. Brownes, the chemist where suspected murderer Doctor John Bodkin-Adam (1899-1983) purchased his poisons. The war memorial was unveiled in November 1920.

Langney Road

This view showing the junction of Terminus Road and Langney Road was taken by my grandmother in 1930. The building in the centre of the view is the Curzon (previously the Picturedrome) Cinema. To the right is Barclays Bank which later became the headquarters of the Eastbourne Building Society from where I obtained my first mortgage.

TERMINUS ROAD. EASTBOURNE

Terminus Road

This view is taken from the opposite angle to the previous pictures. The old postcard was sent in 1904 by a Frenchman who wanted value for his postage! The road seems clear and uncluttered compared to the modern view. T. Knight & Co. on the right were furnisher's and ironmonger's. These shops later became Bobby's department store and are now occupied by Debenhams.

The Millennium Sundial

Prior to the coming of the railway in 1849, Terminus Road was just a footbath that led across fields to the Sea Houses. Today it is a busy pedestrian precinct. The large Portland stone pinnacle is actually a sundial, erected by the Duke of Devonshire to mark the millennium.

Terminus Road

The Gildredge Hotel on the left and nearby Gildredge Road were named after Thomas Gildredge who acquired a part of the Manor of Bourne in 1555. The hotel retains its name but was rebuilt in the 1960s. The building in the centre was previously the Lewes Old Bank but was rebuilt as Barclays in 1958.

Terminus Buildings

This imposing redbrick mansion built in 1900 is situated on the roundabout adjacent to the railway station. In the old view the shops beneath the building are occupied by Pickford's Travel Agents and Pawson's Confectioners but have now been joined to form a popular Italian Restaurant.

South Street

This area was previously called Southbourne and, although mainly Victorian in appearance several houses date from much earlier. On the right is the Dolphin pub, previously the Railway Tavern and nearly opposite the Dew Drop Inn, two more of my teenage haunts.

Eastbourne.   Compton Place Road.   126

Compton Place Road

This road leads north from Meads Road and originally was an access road to Compton Place (page 82). Behind the flint wall on the right is a field which was once known as Saffron's Field and is now the home of both Eastbourne Town Football Club and, since 1884 the home of Eastbourne Cricket Club.

Silverdale Road

Named after one of the estates in Lancashire owned by the Duke of Devonshire. Note the old gas lamp and car on the left. The driver would have needed a driving licence issued by Eastbourne Corporation.

Carlisle Road

Georgina, the eldest daughter of the fifth Duke of Devonshire married the Earl of Carlisle and this, one of the longest roads in Eastbourne, is named after him. The thirty-eight-roomed Alexandra Hotel is on the left of both views. The tower in the old photograph is part of the Devonshire Baths which is where I learnt to swim. The union flag on the new picture flies above the Heritage Centre, which contains a small but fascinating collection of old Eastbourne memorabilia.

CHAPTER 6

Churches

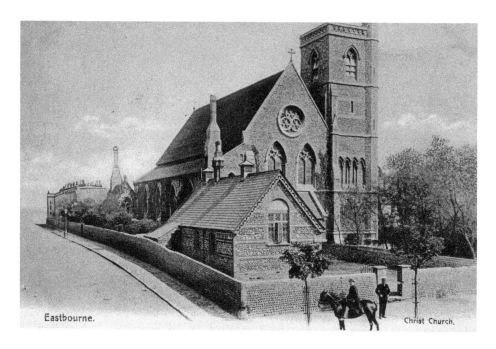

Previous page: The Presbyterian Church in Blackwater Road was built in 1913 and is now St Andrew's United Reformed Church.

Christ Church

This church in Seaside was built in 1859 to the design of Benjamin Ferrey (1810-1880). The author Lewis Carroll (Revd Charles Lutwidge Dodson (1832-1898)) preached here and also visited the nearby Church School. The building in the foreground was Brodie's School where my grandmother Bessie attended as a young girl.

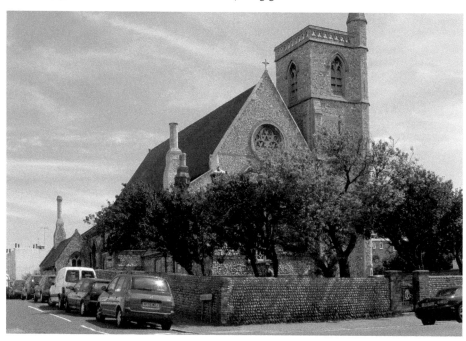

All Souls Church, Eastbourne.

All Souls Church

Situated in Susan's Road, (named after the farm which once stood on this site), the distinctive All Souls Church, was built in just a year in Byzantine style. It is said that the foundations are so deep that there is as much brickwork underground as there is above. The church was funded by Lady Victoria Wellesley, the great-niece of the Duke of Wellington and was consecrated in July 1882. The bell tower is 83 feet (25 metres) tall.

The New Congregational Church

This church is now the Free Church (Countess of Huntingdon Connexion) which is part of a small society of Evangelical Churches with missions in England and Sierra Leone. It was built as the Congregational Church in 1903 on the site of an old forge and was designed by Hastings architect Henry Ward (1854-1927) To the left, Haine's undertakers was built in 1903 although the company was established in 1838.

Ceylon Place

Prior to this church opening in 1871, Baptist worship was conducted at the Leaf Hall in Seaside. In 1943 the row of houses including Lyndhurst House (where the maid is peeking out of the window) was destroyed by enemy action but have been replaced by Busby Court. The church has now been converted into flats.

The Wesleyan School

The Methodists leased a plot of land at the junction of Langney Road and Susans Road from the Duke of Devonshire in 1860. A church was built and in August 1907 (the date of this picture) a hall and school was opened. The architectural critic Nikolas Pevsner described the building as 'churchy'.

CHAPTER 7

Hotels

Previous Page: The Grand Hotel has over 200 rooms and was opened in 1876.

The Cavendish Hotel

This large hotel was designed by Thomas Edward Knightley (1824-1905) in a style that Pevsner describes as 'Frenchy'. In May 1942 a bomb destroyed the east wing of the hotel which was replaced with a modern design. The hotel is named after William Cavendish (the 7th Duke of Devonshire) whose seated statue can be seen in both views.

The Glastonbury Hotel

The picture shows the residents of the hotel in June 1911. The maids and other members of staff are on the upper floor where there is also a lady in bed reading. Today the entrance has been enclosed with double glazing but the decorative ironwork and hanging baskets remain. The hotel is situated on Royal Parade overlooking the beach.

Sussex Hotel
In the seventies the Sussex Hotel in Cornfield Terrace was also pub and I recall the discos in the Lighthouse Bar which could be accessed from Wish Road. The hotel has now been converted into flats and the ground floor is occupied by two popular Italian restaurants.

CHAPTER 8

Other Buildings

WINTER GARDENS, EASTBOURNE   L 300

The Winter Garden

Built of iron, glass and zinc, the Winter Garden (shown on the previous page from the rear) was described, shortly after it was opened in 1875 as being a 'Miniature Crystal Palace'. It was designed by Henry Currey who also designed the Grand Hotel (see page 27). A roller-skating rink here was run by an American, John Calvin Plimpton and on sunny days the doors of the building were opened so that skaters could skate right in!

The Congress Theatre & Towner Art Gallery

The Congress Theatre was opened in 1963 and designed to accommodate 1,678 people. The older photograph was taken around this time when the Fol-De-Rols, a touring variety show, was the main attraction. In 2009 the splendid Towner Gallery was opened adjacent to the theatre. I love the clean lines of this modern building and the modern airy design of the interior.

The Town Hall

In the 1880s Stock's Bank was demolished to make way for the new Town Hall which cost £40,000 (a pound per head of the population). It was designed by Birmingham architect William Tadman-Foulkes and opened in 1886. The tower is 130 feet (40 metres) tall and the clock was installed in 1891 at a cost of £700 by Gillett & Johnston a company established in 1844 and who still maintain the Town Hall clock today.

The Technical Institute

The Technical Institute at the east
end of Grove Road was opened
by the Duchess of Devonshire in
August 1904. It was designed by
Philip Appleby Robson (1871-1951)
and contained a school, library and
museum but was destroyed by enemy
action in June 1943. Eastbourne
Library replaced the institute and was
opened in April 1964.

81

Compton Place

This beautiful building (pictured here from the back) is now a foreign language school. The house was originally built in the 1500s as Bourne Place but in 1724 it was purchased by Spencer Compton, 1st Earl of Wilmington (1673-1743). He was a Speaker of the House of Commons and the second Prime Minister, replacing Walpole in 1742. The state bedroom was built for a proposed visit by George II. He didn't arrive but other royal guests include Edward VII, George V, Queen Mary and our present Queen.

The Tivoli

Today this building looks in a sorry state but it has had a fascinating history. It was opened in 1879 as the New Picture Hall but when the first films were shown here about 1906 it became the Tivoli Cinema. For many years my great uncle, Reginald Gordon was the projectionist. When this picture was taken in 1925 the feature film was *The Kid* starring Charlie Chaplin and to advertise the film my great uncle dressed up as the great actor. A remarkable likeness, I am sure you will agree!

Railway Station

Originally, the railway bypassed Eastbourne and passengers had to travel by road from the nearest station at Polegate. The first train arrived on the new branch line on 14 May 1849 and Eastbourne was never to be the same again. The railway bought holidaymakers by the thousand and the town prospered. This is the third station to be built in the town and it was opened in 1866.

Station Concourse

The red brick railway station was designed by the architect for the London Brighton and South Coast Railway, R. D. Bannister but could he have ever realised that the concourse would have looked as bright and welcoming as it does today? Looking at the same view 100 years ago it appears that the roof may have let in the light but also the rain!

Devonshire Park

The 7th Duke of Devonshire paid for the construction of Devonshire Park which opened on 1 July 1874 in an area of low lying land formerly known as the Wish. The building with the tower is the back of the Devonshire Park Theatre opened in 1884. To the right is the Winter Garden and (in the modern picture) the Congress Theatre (see pages 78-9).

Devonshire Park, Eastbourne

56938

Tennis in the Park

Devonshire Park was originally intended to be a Cricket Ground and indeed turf from the old ground near Terminus Road was re-laid here. The first tennis courts were laid out in 1879, just two years after the Lawn Tennis Association standardised the rules of the game. The first major tennis tournament was held here in 1881 and today the venue is used for many major competitions, including (in 2010) the Davis Cup.

EASTBOURNE

The Clifton Hotel

Situated in South Street, the Clifton Hotel was built in 1888 on the site of the Clifton School whose headmaster, Revd Edward Ebenezer Crake was vicar of Jevington Church and the author of several historical works including a history of Herstmonceux Castle. The building was later renamed the Greenwich Hotel and has now been converted into shops and flats.

Kings Drive

The District General Hospital was built in 1976 and has over 500 beds and 8 operating theatres. It was built on land adjacent to the old Rodmill Farm alongside Kings Drive which was originally an access road to Hampden Park which was purchased by the council in 1901. In the old view, Rodmill Farm can be seen on the left and the site of the DGH on the right with the village of Willingdon on the horizon.

The Salvation Army

It is difficult to imagine but the Salvation Army band were responsible for the formation of the Eastbourne Police. During the 1880s they insisted on marching through the town every Sunday and playing hymns on the seafront despite the fact that this was contrary to by-laws. On one occasion, 7,000 people took to the streets to protest but the disturbances turned nasty and were sometimes described as riots. Thirty-nine members of the Salvation Army were sent to prison and the Council acted by establishing its own Police Force in 1891. The picture shows the band in 1904 standing outside their Citadel in Langney Road.

CHAPTER 9

Murder!

1782 EASTBOURNE. South Cliff Avenue.

Previous page: The Police Station in Latimer Road built in 1895.

A Policeman Murdered

As Countess Sztaray left her house at 6, South Cliff Avenue (indicated by an asterisk on the old photograph) on 9 October 1912 she noticed a man trying to break into an upper window. She telephoned the police and Police Inspector Walls was sent to investigate. He called up at the man *"here old chap – come down"* but was answered by two shots from a revolver and he died quickly. The police station received another frantic call from the house *"There is a murder being done – send someone on a bicycle!"*

FUNERAL PROCESSION OF P. INSPECTOR WALLS EASTBOURNE. 16/10/12.

The Murderer

The murderer was George MacKay alias John Williams who was executed having been found guilty at Lewes prison. Inspector Arthur Walls, who had served in the Police for twenty-four years, was buried on 16 October 1912. It was a massive funeral with a parade through the town centre (seen here passing Terminus Road) when many resident stood silently to watch. Over £600 was raised by the public for his widow who also received a pension from the town council.

The Crumble Murder

In April 1924 the discovery of a bloodstained knife at Waterloo Station led detectives to a remote cottage on the Crumbles to the east of Eastbourne, a site now occupied by the Sovereign Harbour development. Patrick Mahon had taken his girlfriend Emily Kaye to the cottage for a romantic tryst which ended in her death. In a panic Mahon cut the body into small pieces. Blood hounds were called in to help to discover the gruesome remains.